Edinburgh
7/53

Every good wish Jean my darling,

Fitz

Christmas 1944

TEN SUMMERS

by the same author

poems

DISPERSAL POINT
BEYOND THIS DISREGARD
SOUTH OF FORTY

fiction

JACOBSON'S LADDER
AND LASTLY THE FIREWORKS
UNCLE ARTHUR AND OTHER STORIES

non-fiction

THE GREEN GRASS GREW ALL ROUND
WHO ONLY ENGLAND KNOW

J L
THE BODLEY HEAD

John Pudney

TEN SUMMERS

poems

[1933—1943]

London
John Lane the Bodley Head

First published 1944

Printed in Great Britain by
UNWIN BROTHERS LIMITED, LONDON AND WOKING
for JOHN LANE THE BODLEY HEAD LIMITED
8 Bury Place, London, W.C. 1.

IF there is such a thing as war-poetry, the making of this selection from ten years of my work has taught me that I have been writing war-poetry all the time. The contents are taken from "Spring Encounter" published by Methuen, "Open the Sky" published by Boriswood—both volumes being now blitzed or out of print—and from the three volumes of verse ("Dispersal Point," "Beyond This Disregard" and "South of Forty") published during the war by The Bodley Head. Some new poems have been added. My thanks to my friends Desmond Hawkins and Wilfred Hanchant for looking over my shoulder while the choice was made.

J. P.

For C. S. P.

Contents

First Drums Heard

[1933]

HOW will I hold myself,
　　How will I keep my stance,
Now at the frontier of commonsense,
Now I am faced about
To meet my chance?

Is it much easier
To hold on with one's fear,
To grip a rifle in the frightened air,
Crouched on the knees
To wait the word to fire?

Would it be better thus
With little more explained
Than where artillery is being trained,
How to put on a mask
If gas is in the wind?

It would be simple surely,
Hero in all opinions,
To accept discipline in the battalions
Safe in the company
Of fearing millions?

How will I stand apart
How will I keep my stance
In the dark crisis of the present tense,
When I am face to face
With every chance?

Crossing

[1933]

STARTING at night
I watched a crane and tackle,
The burden of ship's muffled cargo loaded:
The group ashore, the group upon the ship,
Shouts and curt understanding
Lip to lip.

Waiting, apart,
I loaded another burden,
Heard the impatient siren in my heart:
Created, knew the purpose of it harden.

Events

[1933]

FELLOW man, happy at day's end, fire's border,
　It is to you, unwelcome I come a hinter,
Searching, intolerable in your order,
For spring recoiled and diligent in winter.
Fireside man, I demand uncomfortable lovers,
Refusal of willing arms. I have you believe
News, wirelessed, how the ghostly squadron hovers,
Forcing the eye. Now may your hands achieve
Not the scramble for safety, the fluttered blind,
But a bleak tryst out at the mouth of the estuary.
Are you afraid of darkness, of looking behind?
Daylight will never give you sanctuary:
Seasons will never change in the closed land, the mind:
The last spring fallow fail, unkind.

Source

[1933]

HERE at original source, in water meadows
    Here I have retreated, am pacing it to and fro,
Testing a tendon, trying a muscle's ease,
Watching the Thames, its quickening silver division,
Knowing its flowing, paces, swift approaches,
And bridges, whirlpools, arches and hesitations,
How it will become tidal.

Now it is April, metal the skies, taut over, steep above
Awakened orchards, cornlands.
Branches, the bearing wood pointing all pointing growth,
Bending in sapling strength
Braced with the wind's strict tension.
And the roan mare, her fullness anxious now,
Is pacing careful, wary of her foaling.

Now it is plain: here avenues, ways begin,
April to June, river to tidal basin,
This summer's crop and new stock on the farm.
This is where I, abashed to hesitate,
In eagerness must pause, and O my love,
Certain that I must gather strength, with you
Tidal become, the traffic way for ships.

Heirs

[1933]

ALLOTTED hours
We slept 'tween factory hooters;
Or used our time
Admiring, making notes
Of scores and scares and crimes,
Amused at vestiges
Of customs and old tunes
That died in villages.

Inheritors
Of that dishonoured country,
We sloped our mouths,
Spoke slantwise man to man,
As if we feared guns trained
Across great distances;
Uncertain where they aimed,
Taking no chances.

Perhaps in Spring

[1933]

PERHAPS in spring
As rumour goes in towns
Lifting a leg of whispers at street corners,
As gossip among cleaners
Who hesitate at doors
And congregate on stairs
Telling the count of family misdemeanours.

Perhaps in February and a changing sky
With hail still frozen in between the snow drops,
Explicit in the tree-tops
What we have had in mind
Shall be upon the wind:
And what were our night time hopes shall start upon
    all lips.

Like that at first
As spring makes a beginning
As the stiff twigs that click in their uprightness
In the wood's winter darkness
Break into curt salute
Announce in brilliant shoot
Their certainties, renewal of their brightness.

All we who dream
Watch for a break in towns
At bridges, parks, street corners for revival,
Swallows, their rearrival,
Find us O wide awake
Speaking, again to speak,
Join the column of dancers in carnival.

Over His Shoulder

[1933]

AM I to live that kind of life again
    Pitting despair against despair, awake
In sombre dawns, aware in afternoons?
In all respects like all the other damned
A dawn scrapes shadows off or day's decline
To zero hour compels to further action,
One of the mercenaries sick for home
Fighting a rearguard action against forces
Better equipped, convinced their cause's justice?
If I am hemmed again by sudden bayonets
Jabbing demands, surrender upon terms
I will die pitilessly in the mud,
Foothold at least, basis for stronger footsteps.

Open the Sky

[1934]

BEYOND our strongest squadron's range
Whom do I envy, O what high prestige
Stranger than gods that still the hearts of boys?
Had I your purpose who affirm a course,
With lifting wind, accelerating engines, rise,
I could soar with you in your universe.

Open the sky! So charted are the spheres,
They are as known as calculated days
Or years that mark their passage in a face.
You are impatient for your journey, I
For a sparse house, for living, for increase
Scanted by winter as the growing trees.

Fertile

[1934]

ALL these are fertile,
  Grip the spring air:
Peach, pear and cherry blossom
Strain in thirsty light.

Integrity of trees,
This pink and white
Bright splendour of increase
Disturb my peace!

Drench my inquisitive body,
Lips to drink,
Eyes to devise
And limbs in such immaculate wonder
To have speech, to think!

Resort

[1934]

AGELESS men, behind terraces,
   Glance over geraniums,
Calling for Vichy water
In the long afternoons.

Girls, as tender as cats for milk,
Are framed in doorways
Decorating their small tight cheeks
In clots and dabs.

Men and girls are coupled
By painted fingernails
By car cushions
By the new tune called "Love".

Song of a Million Spring Evenings

[1935]

NOW dip your fingers in the blood:
For Christ is dead. The bannered spring
Laughs for the deed, if deed it was,
To mock the man and kill the king.

The king lies dead, the king in man.
Close but your eyes, you will see now
The gibbett and the crucifix
Sprout bud and green like every bough.

The buses run in Gibbett Lane:
And Saturday, on Cheap Parade
The shopping women shove their prams.
The money made, the price is paid.

The rent is paid; and football lads
Pay eighteenpence to watch the game.
Quick bets are made in alleyways.
The price of beer is kept the same.

The same kids squeal in Angel Row.
The usual mothers are in bed.
Bearing, this time of year, the spring,
And number ten's inside her, dead.

The dead, they say, don't need to eat:
But dead men cannot work or play.
Dead women are too cold to love
Or suffer in a family way.

Nobody speaks of death just now,
In Bitter Square, nobody speaks,
More than to pass the time of day,
And nod toward the passing weeks:

Which day the pay to spend on life,
Which day the rent-collector comes,
The eye must calculate to live,
Doing the necessary sums.

Say not aloud: 'these two make four'.
The deafened streets will overhear,
Be careful not to raise your voice,
To say, 'this time next month, next year'.

Now is the anguish of the spring
And blood is on your bloody hands.
The deed you mocked is in this earth;
Pray that his blood run through your lands:

Blood to enrich and stain the soil,
The darker for the sacrifice,
Pray you the keener rain may come
To calm the fever of your eyes.

Saturday night the hero boys
Stand out beneath the yellow lights
With ready eyes to con the girls
Whom each beneath the skin invites.

The fifteen seats and thirty trees,
Down in the War Memorial Park
Commemorate the shape of love
Secured by Corporation dark.

And then, young only once, the young
Are waiting in the Picture queue,
Each in his turn to mount the stairs
To paradise to get the view.

You who have touched the blood of Christ
After the laughter, after pain,
I seek your pity, not remorse.
    I seek your eyes in God again.

I seek your pity, your man's eye,
Your woman's touch, who will not share
The rotten bed of paradise,
Living in Bitter Square.

Landing

[1935]

HERE drifted flesh, and drowned bone, and
    unknown
Fabulous sea-foliage are washed upon the sand:
Here, in this brilliant land,
My eyes perceive no shadow but their own.

The moon conspires and swings. The ocean's dearth
Is broken with resistance to the shape
Of promontory and cape,
To the stationary pattern of the earth.

Living and dying here are equal, each
Adamantly met and friended. Here my eyes,
Perceiving how the final substance dies,
Hurry across the margin of the beach,
But find the safe boats out of reach.

Riviera

[1935]

YOUNG men and girls,
In postures of inertia,
Scribble in the sand
With soft bronzed fingers.

At noon, some of the girls
Sigh, wishing they were waves:
But the men admire
The foreshortening of their own bodies.

They dance together,
Patiently, in the sunless evenings,
Safe from the old beach, the old seas,
The old ship's gear.

Spanish Coast

[1935]

HOW finely death, in this caress of air,
   Stinks with the rotten sifting of blown sand,
Like a cripple among running children or the idiot's
   stare
At laughter and the dancing. Here I lay my hand,
Lightly, to the tackle, to the capstans, boats
Bright with the surf and keen as weather-eye,
To wicker gear, the fish traps, and the cork bark floats.
These are kind to touch; these satisfy.
For with the coiling of a line, the mending of the net,
I smell men's quick-as-water-ripple skin,
Old invaders, Africa and Greece, the footprints wet
With death in the next wave flowing in.

The Long Night

[1936]

ANNA in a close dream: and my waked heart hears
The hurraying of stars, the windy white light cheers,
And, closer, the close argument of which a part
Is in Anna's dreaming heart and in my heart.

Waking alone: O wishing the earth the less
For the wakeful bone, for the blinded wakefulness
Which points to twisted gutters, to the long street's
    bend
As the end of a mean city which has no end,
Which does not dare to be cheered by the stars nor
    dare
Brave sunrise in the blinded street's despair,

Leaf

[1936]

WITH a maternal image; with autumnal ease
   Of the trees' surrender, wind in the living trees;
With a river's tidal flush and the slow fall
Of the burden to the sea; I am that tall.
I have that measure, notch in the wall.

Measure not love and the joy that eye gives eye
When the boughs' jet fingers scrawl the winter sky,
For the lover's laughter changes in this bed;
Green leaf is dead; all, back to the root, is dead.
Measure not love, the heart, the head.

With a mother's eye choose this, the joy of the less,
The sweet kiss and the end's sharp accent; tenderness
Is the knowing of the loss, the season's quiet break.
What your hand has made, your heart must take and
   make.
Dead leaf is loosened and the wind will shake.

Song

[1937]

THE youthful amorist makes hay
And sneers at passionate pursuits,
Discovering the only way
To lick his proud new boots.

The libertine, reformed and wise,
Bores with old jokes and new hygiene.
The educated theorise
And stay divinely clean.

The puritan is not the fool,
Nor the devoted sensualist,
But so much data learnt at school
And later found not to exist.

The lover full of anarchy,
So thoroughly disdains the laws,
He lives and dies a mystery
Without apparent cause.

Reading Room,
Salford Public Library

[1937]

NO eagle eye will find him: no quick jest,
　Over his shoulder, will deceive
His solitary trust. It would be best
To leave a note for him, and leave.

It would not do to mention him by name;
Nor question him upon his views;
Too many of his answers are the same,
Too many words confuse.

So with his trust—he and the million more
For whom tomorrow brings no flowers,
No winners, dinners, fortune in the draw—
Let him sleep out the timeless hours.

Industrial Landscape

[1937]

NOT Satan but a booted merchant stood,
    God-fearing, God-important, in this street:
Desiring profit and a livelihood.
The earth obedient to his pacing feet
Worked out in mines, clamped down with cobble stones,
Rich money, profits, the soil's sullen juice
Sucked up its favour, fat upon his bones,
As he improved the yield by skilful use.

This is not Satan's edifice and city:
Not a far-sighted Satan's gain:
This damned ignored, subject of hope and pity
Of casual Christians passing in the train.
This is the gain, the conquest of a man,
Heir to the trodden acres of the ground
Our booted merchant strutted with his plan.
His profit, if not safe, is still as sound.

In the North

[1937]

BEHIND this wall
  Winter will also fall
Obliterating nothing in its throes
For nothing grows.

Nor will life wake
For the first drifted flake
And when the snow's fast innocence hides shame
This house will be the same.

Nothing is lost.
The skeleton stands fast.
Though winter hide and thawing spring reveal:
Here, season will not heal.

Going Back There

[1937]

THE boyish cockcrow, or the first
   Sharp midnight, in the heart, destroy
A momentary poet's thirst
And substitute the boy.

The single boy, the callow sense
Of the warm meadow and the jay,
Whose speckled sound experience
Kept warily away.

The night the dead rose, daisy-eyed,
The muscles fleshed upon their bones,
We graveyard lovers pressed aside
The green from graven stones:

How the dead gazed and stood apart,
And how they whispered in the grass,
The lover with his broken heart,
Villagers and upper class.

Their sinning flesh had fed the yew,
Their pale sweat made the bluebell sleek,
Out of their rot the green sheets grew,
The pillow for love's cheek.

But now the native's memory shrinks
From the sought country scene.
The word he thought, the word he thinks
Is stifled in the green,

Is sucked into the grasses root,
Into the wax within the stem.
The new ghosts jostle for the earthly fruit:
And silently each thought is snatched by them.

The Mountain

[1937]

THERE'S death in this, brother, in the mountain
Seeming near and dearer now than all,
Than dusted hearth, the football, or the dahlias
Against the backyard wall.

Men yet may give their treasure for the mountain,
Halving luck and love: but there is shame
In the illusion of its worth and wonder.
Death here, brother, by another name.

High Wood

[1937]

LONELY, as at thought's end, in this placid country
 Marches the wood, where the alarmist pheasants start
At twig-break, wind-rustle, or an explosion
Of cold-eyed sportsmen. Here my heart—
No less ready than these men with laughter
Sauntering the alleys, their cold eyes
Jovially aimed against the flight of pheasants—
Here stands still beneath the tranquil skies.

Gluttonous, the worms ignore our breathing,
Ignorant of summer gloss gone from the grass,
And the tilled earth shifts, easily, without motion.
This is the time that will never pass:
Not when lurid noons lean down upon the steeples,
When frightened tradesmen shutter out the hours,
When the drowned seamen float far from the bridges,
When wooden crosses rot among the flowers.

Gravely the woods, the water-meadows, and the
    pollards.
Wait upon innocent lovers' ease,
Whose memories will be painted with the shadows
Of water, the wood, the trees.
No less will my heart hold this memorial,
This halted time by the wood,
To watch youth come and age go in the alleys,
And, like a god, to have wished them good.

The Distressed Area

[1938]

THE wind leans on this house. The hags ride out,
   Neighing their welcome to ill-luck, to lack,
To waste, wind-provender, dreg, dottle, clout,
To sunken belly and bare back.

Sweep the gaunt yards clean, sweep the dark ways,
Scratch the doomed silence with your bleak new
      brooms.
You add no more days to our stated days:
Nor clean you our soiled rooms.

These walls inhabited by life are all you own,
Paid for by rent. But where I lodge I keep
The furniture of flesh, the marrow in the bone.
That dirt you may not sweep.

The wind leans on this house. Winter is passed
In watching the shrunk light, the encompassed seed
Pressed in by native soil, held fast
In the fast silence of the season's need.

Nights arrogant with owls, hags horsed on fears,
Boss-eyed in haunted alleys, hungry-jawed,
Lend a momentum to the minute: but the years
Find the same skeleton unawed.

Unbroomed, unwasted in the black days' blast,
Such dust or dross or bone or flesh or voice
Of this, the tenant of this starving house, at last
Shall seek the spring as a bride of choice:

Shall force a festival out of the year
Which casts a chuck and ripens in the eye.
Dirt buried in the soil, in rooms, in fear,
Shall all uncovered in the white wind lie.

A Prey to Innocence

[1938]

ALL day he listened to the children's voices,
   Thinking of children, light without a shadow,
White light, cast lavishly on latch and lintel,
Soaking the walls of all the narrow houses.

A prey to innocence, to voices, faces,
Innocently starting, hurting, loving, lying,
All day he waited eager as a virgin,
Roused by green corn and every possible lover.

Epitaph

[1938]

HE will have drawn his blanket close
   Upon the glory that he owns.
Pray you there may be warmth enough
Who lie among his bones.

He may have wrung a tiny warmth
Beneath the wide world's horizon,
Yet you will find bare ground more kind
Than lying with his skeleton.

Civilized Man

[1 9 3 9]

I SHALL take more killing than you think,
Who bind my body with your chains,
For I am young and old as yew, nor shrink
From wind blast or the cruel rains.

I, who am soft as woman, tender·
As the first smile in the bed,
Who have shouted in the spring, caressed the slender
Stalk, the sensible head.

I shall take more killing than you think,
Who think the beautiful lives of men crushed out,
In lead, and slime and stink
Of agony and petrol, make a final rout.

The Dead Airmen

[1 9 4 0]

I

WHEN tranquil hours shall come as sure as leaf,
And only love shall spoil the heart's good ease,
When weariness has drained the guilt and grief,
When, sure as winter, death falls; think of these,
These young and easy of heart, the single
Of hand and skilful ones who seek not death
In livid hours where past and future mingle,
Where live men petrify and dead catch breath.
The victim gods in an heroic age,
These ride like thunder where man's fear and greed
Are frontiers interlocked in mean outrage;
These fly, now engined by all human need.
These, wishing life, must range the falling sky,
Whom an heroic moment calls to die.

II

YOU shall have your revenge who flew and died,
Spending your daylight before day began.
You shall have good hours back: and go in pride
Against the dark. Protagonist of man,
Account shall be for lives in measured days.
You shall inherit hours which are replaced,
The earth won back, the trustier human ways
From history recovered, on them based
An amplitude of noble life. Prelude
Shall there be none: nor count of other cost
Of dying, living, loving. Oh intrude
Your lively innocent ghosts upon the frost
Of present winter, quickening in its dearth.
Your vengeance shall be spring upon the earth.

III

A SORRY world, bereft of simple tongue
       Had not a word for honour, saved its smile
For the philosopher and wished the young
The idiot happiness, the decent pile.
Peace was this troubled bargain, though some tried
To fix the brokers in the market, some
Dared to consider how the prices lied,
And bought insurance for the doom to come.
Yet none had simple speech for simple deed
And none could match the action with the soul;
Until you lived, and died in taking heed
Of duty and a routine job; till whole
You grew and served. So honour may be said
To be the decent shroud to serve the dead.

I V

IF men with lives to lose have any luck
  The bell will toll for them another day.
Lucky are they who hear this hour struck,
Impatient while the minutes slip away
To lean again upon the roomy air,
With brief regrets, but loving life the more
And lovelier for life. Who shall prepare
An order of the day which shall restore
The finer temper to the man, to break
Bright generous sun upon the human frame
Choosing not whom it fire or whom it wake
By whispering to each timid soul by name?
Pray God shall raise such honour and such skill
When orders are to live and not to kill.

Combat Report

[1 9 4 0]

*J*UST *then I saw the bloody Hun.*
 You saw the Hun? You, light and easy,
Carving the soundless daylight. *I was breezy*
When I saw that Hun. Oh wonder,
Pattern of stress, of nerve poise, flyer,
Overtaking time. *He came out under*
Nine-tenths cloud, but I was higher.
Did Michael Angelo aspire,
Painting the laughing cumulus, to ride
The majesty of air. *He was a trier*
I'll give him that, the Hun. So you convert
Ultimate sky to air speed, drift, and cover:
Sure with the tricky tools of God and lover.
I let him have a sharp four-second squirt,
Closing to fifty yards. He went on fire.
Your deadly petals painted, you exert
A simple stature. Man-high, without pride,
You pick your way through heaven and the dirt.
He burnt out in the air: that's how the poor sod died.

Dispersal Point

[1 9 4 1]

I DID not trust myself to know your names;
Nor dare to let you touch my coward heart.
I overheard the others call you James,
That you were good at games,
That you were in it from the start.

Apart you fly. You, with a surgeon's glance,
Grave and discriminate, enforce the dreams
Of mathematic theory. You advance,
From probable extremes,
To take a human chance.

A girl with laughing lips can make you cry;
You have been saving money for a car:
You never tell your mother where you fly:
Keeping your station in the sky:
Solitary cunning star.

Apostolic name, no hero, fellow
Mother's son whose secret is life only.
This is the coward's heart which does not know
How to laugh and let you go,
How to answer you, the lonely.

Convoy Job

[1 9 4 1]

CONVOY the dead:
   Those humble men who drown,
Dreaming of narrow streets, of alleys snug
In lamplight, love in a furrowed bed,
Pints in a Rose and Crown.

Escort the brave
Whose hearts, unsatisfied
With the kind stairs and tender hearths of love,
Are loyal to the cunning of the wave,
The sparse rule of the tide.

Fly over these,
Humble and brave, who sail
And trim the ships with very life; whose lives
Delineate the seas.
Patrol their deathless trail.

Air Gunner

[1 9 4 1]

THE eye behind this gun made peace
  With a boy's eye which doubted, trembled,
Guileless in the mocking light
Of frontiers where death assembled.

Peace was as single as the dawn,
Flew straightly as the birds migrating,
Timelessly in tune with time,
Purposeful, uncalculating.

So boyish doubt was put away:
The man's eye and the boy's were one.
Mockery and death retreat
Before the eye behind this gun.

So I Praise These

[1941]

DO not suppose
   The amazing daffodil has thrust
From the waste plot
Or the polluted dust.

Nor was the soil
From which a gallantry of roses flowered,
Luckless, unhusbanded,
By God or mankind soured.

So I praise these,
The gallant, the amazing, who from chance
Of birth or circumstance
This darker hour enhance.

In praising them
I celebrate a soil which is still sweet
In mine and mill,
In meadow and in street.

The Dusk Take-off

[1 9 4 1]

COMPASS wise and cunning in your calculation,
  Skilled in stress, in limbering the machine,
Deadly in armament, you, through a perspex
Face the European scene.

Where lost men start up from their sleep to hear
Your passage fabulous as starry hosts:
Where dreamers claw the twilight of the dream
Which pins them to their own live ghosts.

Human, no manlier, better than man may be,
Without more claim to happiness than home,
Than loving hands, than laughter in a village,
The job on an aerodrome,

Where, heedless of a cosmic strategy,
You learn the cool bright tactics, where the air
Is mastered in the throes of man's despair:
There choose to live and dare.

Security

[1 9 4 1]

EMPTY your pockets, Tom, Dick and Harry,
  Strip your identity; leave it behind.
Lawyer, garage-hand, grocer, don't tarry
With your own country, your own kind.

Leave all your letters. Suburb and township,
Green fen and grocery, slip-way and bay,
Hot-spring and prairie, smoke stack and coal tip,
Leave in our keeping while you're away.

Tom, Dick and Harry, plain names and numbers,
Pilot, observer, and gunner depart.
Their personal litter only encumbers
Somebody's head, somebody's heart.

Release Till Dawn

[1941]

IT is not easy to be strict and calm,
   To satisfy the heart and show a care
Where cares are coins jingled in the palm,
The price of cigarettes, a pint, a fare
To a resort from time. Who shall prepare
The remedy for us, specific balm,
For the anatomy which war lays bare,
For wounded pity and for unhealed qualm?
As leaf in season and, as season, sure
There is no summer now; and words must seem
A sleight of hand, at best the huckster's cure,
Quick pattered from the kerb. The very theme
Of words are leaves where leaves cannot endure:
And action is more ready than is dream.

For Johnny

[1941]

DO not despair
    For Johnny-head-in-air;
He sleeps as sound
As Johnny underground.

Fetch out no shroud
For Johnny-in-the-cloud;
And keep your tears
For him in after years.

Better by far
For Johnny-the-bright-star,
To keep your head,
And see his children fed.

Air Crew

[1 9 4 1]

NOT bunting, band, loudspeaker speech
    Nor touch-line followers exhort
The lonely ones who each to each
By intercom report.

Disciple of the wind, discern
The language of good faith which they
Together, solitary, learn
Who order and obey.

The lively discipline of trees
The confines of an aircraft house:
And you may earn who fly with these
A harmony of boughs.

The bough has life, the tree is good,
And strictly is the outline drawn:
For thus is freedom understood,
Manhood most proudly worn.

Waterborne Balloon Barrage

[1 9 4 1]

COME paint the dawn with dainty elephants,
    To graze upon the pastures of the sky,
Limpidly to crop ice blades of air,
Dumb and dangerous and sly.

From the bright salver of the estuary
Substantial with a violet snipe, pale geese
Muscular and energetic, see
The barrage float at peace.

And patiently its minders, pioneers
In a preposterous logic, weather-eyed,
Drill the grave elephantine flock
Poised on the eternal tide.

Ballad of Jack Overdue

[1 9 4 1]

COME back, come back, Jolly Jack Straw.
    There's ice in the killer sea.
Weather at base closes down for the night:
And the ash-blonde Waaf is waiting tea.

How many long Atlantic hours
Has he hunted there alone:
Has he trimly weaved on the silent air
The dullest patrol that's ever flown.

How can they know he found at last
That he made a hunter's strike:
And swooped on a sly swift shark as it dived:
Saw gouting oil mount carpet-like.

Jolly Jack Straw is beating it back,
But his wireless set is blown.
He cannot report his long-sought luck,
Or the ice-dark blinding the eye and bone.

Come back, come back, Jolly Jack Straw,
For the ash-blonde Waaf drinks tea;
And the tea leaves tell her fortune as well.
Come back, come back from the killer sea.

Man Alive

[1 9 4 1]

ENOUGH of death!
  It looms too large in words:
And those who die
Know but the death of birds.

Enjoy the sky,
Possess the field of air,
Cloud be your step,
The west wind be your stair.

This province range,
Familiar of the sun.
The birds' strict life
Demands your stricter one.

Under your eye
The easy tits await
Hand pressure cool,
The wrist dispassionate.

But man alive,
By no horizon bound,
Unfenced, unroofed,
Old roots hold in the ground.

The WAAF Corporal

[1941]

CORPORAL Alice dances like aspen:
  And life is long
As the life of a leaf.
Corporal Alice chooses not often:
And not from love
Shall she come to grief.

Now all you sweethearts whisper with Alice
And all you wives
Smile close in the dance.
Somebody's mother answers with Alice:
And lucky lives
Are blessed by her glance.

Corporal Alice dances off duty:
And life is brief
As the life of the flowers.
Corporal Alice shall keep her beauty
Longer than leaf
Than war's lost hours,

Dream Under Fire

[1 9 4 1]

WHERE the moon sheds her clothes of sin:
   Where the salt tides are frozen dry:
And the indifferent hours begin
Everlastingly to spin.

Where diamonds take the place of hearts,
Worn round the neck not on the sleeve:
Where the anatomy of parts
Is keenest of the arts.

Where democrats and millionaires
And beggars swell the noonday rut,
To seek provision for their heirs,
Lest midnight take them unawares.

Here do not speak of permanence,
Where the moon sheds her clothes of sin,
You have not saved the magic pence
Of an heir's inheritance.

Here destiny I play as stake,
Where diamonds take the place of hearts,
And love is not a glass, to break
With bomb, barrage or earthquake.

Night Fighter Patrol

[1 9 4 2]

HEREDITARY gestures, through the bone
   Of rigid time and timeless flesh, derive
Likeness more final than the graven stone,
Than history more alive.

Now, in the cockpit, smile or flick your wrist,
Study the compass, glance across the main
Of tideless night. In such features exist
The fortunes of your strain.

The sailor's son or shop-bred boy or one
Whose people farmed hard acres share the style,
The faithful glance, the lively skeleton
Scaling the steep night with a smile.

Toast

[1 9 4 2]

WHO live in hope and hope to live;
   And give too much and always give:
Who die too often and contrive
To look alive and love alive:
Who con the lonely pulse of life.
Here's "Happy Landings" to the Wife.

The Bomb Dump

[1 9 4 2]

HERE shall we make a pact
And for the time compose
A heart too quick to act,
An eye too slow to close.

These patient bombs await,
As grocer's goods on shelves,
A hand which shall relate
Them to ourselves.

Death in such racks and rows
Never more neatly schemes
To stun the heart that knows,
The eye that dreams.

Stroke the insensible skin
Or bravely chalk your joke,
Your message to Berlin,
And fun shall be our cloak.

If pity would relent,
If manhood be unmanned,
Keep warm in this garment
And chilly jokes withstand.

Nocturne: The Mess

[1 9 4 2]

WE do not say good-bye:
    We play no game of hearts:
Eyes too often lie.
Let's play darts.

Tom, Dick and Harry nod:
We don't say what we think:
And, not being God,
Let's have a drink.

To sentimentalize
Men lifting up the latch
Starts the old false ties.
Got a match?

Easier, without friends,
Without the secret game,
Nothing starts or ends.
What's your name?

The Blind

[1 9 4 2]

TO be alive like Sam,
    Sam balancing his beer
Upon his chin:
Sam somersaulting past the chandelier,
Performing his flat spin.

To be alone like Sam
Would be to watch the place
Of Ropey Jack,
To miss the concord of that bastard's face
Who isn't coming back.

Spring, 1942

[1 9 4 2]

NO longer separated by the fireside tale,
   By the gaggling teachers, by the pages
Of maturer taste, the sober history:
No longer out of arms' length, out of eyes' reach,
Dressed in the homespun purple of the psalmist,
Clothed in the sacrificial light of the recorder:
Men find a cause to die for: and the bravery
Of this riper spring, unjust and harmful,
Scalds the wide open eye and sears the tongue.
Men find a cause to die for: and so chance to live,
Humble in the blast, or in the lightning
Royally assume the gait of heroes.
Only when the firing squad about-turns;
The rescue party goes home; the sailor home
Hangs up his cap; when airmen in careful creases queue
At a manager's frosted door. Then all is lost.
Death's no respecter in this unjust spring,
No chooser under the callous rain: but, brothers,
All is won when men, who find a cause to die for, live.

Flying Fortresses

[1 9 4 2]

FLYING with Americans in their B Seventeen,
  Weapon-bright ship of the new world, the steady
Majestic job, I saw my England green,
Rutted, furrowed and smudged already
With history and war and the loved scene.
There below, framed in the bombardier's panel,
Was harvest stooked, or the eighteenth century plan
Of ancestors, or pitheads, or a glint of the Channel,
Or plush-bricked manufacturing town. A man
In American kit beside me, all that crew,
Positive all, teamed-up in their B Seventeen
Out of the scalding west of America, anew
Brought, quick and keen, rare passion to the view.

Rank and File

[1942]

*Written upon the 450th anniversary of the first sight-
ing of land by Rodrigo de Triana, a seaman in one
of the caravels accompanying Christopher Columbus*

ONE held the New World in his eye,
  Treasure beyond the gold and Indians his pocket yearned.
Rodrigo de Triana was his name,
Seaman in *Nina*, one of the caravels.
Little I know of him. For all his fame
Is the name of him, centuries in print,
By this chance earned.

Did he grow old, bearing that image,
The New World, land seen on a Friday?
Did he tell the tale: "It was October,
The twelfth of the month, in the morning . . ."?

Out of the alleys and arches and inns of Europe,
Such sailed with handiness and seaman skill,
Plighting here love and there goodwill,
Familiars to whom a story could be told
Of America, rarer than Indians and gold.

Rodrigo, Rodrigo, seaman look-out,
The New World held in his eye;
Unlettered, tongue-tied, in the European triumph

For Don Columbus under the hot royal sky.
Upon what tide of chance and humble fortune
—A sailor's, soldier's, airman's treasure in his head—
Nothing in hand, did he yield his body to a last sea-bed!

Leaving a kiss or a name in print or sons so bred
Gladly to ride the elements, not for a tale to be told
Of America, Europe or gold,
But because the eye is wide and blood is red.

Memorial

[1942]

FOR those who leave no trace,
　Their heirs these times:
For those unlovely heroes:

For those whose fingers fall
On iron for love,
On weariness for pillows:

For those whose laughter went
Out with the light
In any evening's danger:

For young and old who die
At every hour
Now life is sole and solemn monument.

The Party

[1 9 4 2]

THE heart cries out
  For seeing them, the chance
Trick of the light, or the exuberance
Single as dawn-sky, or the sad
Swig of an evening with the luckless lad.

Let us be plain,
Our words against the dark
Be fleet and brittle as the vaulting spark,
Ash-still by daylight though it be.
The heart cries out for all the head must see.

Like black frost, fell
And murderous to flowers,
Are these, death's whimsical, unstable hours
That spare or strike. So fast and black
Our times are ice-locked in by loss, by lack.

But for such souls,
Some luckless, some expert,
Within whom strives the fury and the hurt,
Who prop the sky with light, and doom
Greet innocently in the whole air's room.

To the Bomber Pilot in Doubt

[1942]

Nimble destroyer!
  May you come to build,
In space sucking and swelling with Satanic might,
Steel-fast patrols tempered against the night
Behind men's eyes.

Present ambition
May be soon fulfilled—
Fear's face the back of your hand, your answer gay,
Rinsing the daylight out of day.
But grown more wise
In this beginning
Of strict and testing trust,
Navigating chaos, searching the utmost end,
By discipline of deed your tasks extend
Beyond death and the dust.

Beyond reprisal,
The mean killing, the unjust
Abasement of body and spirit, your intent,
Eager for life simply, may still be bent
To courses ordering the firmament.

No Summer Now

[1 9 4 2]

O FROST fell early
  Upon the flowering bough.
There is no summer now.

It is a story
As old as any they tell
How, still as death, frost fell.

How life was lovely
As life was never before
And will be never more.

Though season surely
Follows the season now spent
And fills man with content.

O frost falls early,
Old as time is the sorrow
Killed or cured tomorrow.

Beneath the Aiming Sky

[1942]

SHALL I write us a patriotic poem,
　Like a flower that takes on colour
Before the aiming gun?
Shall I write of home and of love of country,
Of a football pitch or a river
All ample in the sun?

I could write of the English speech and cadence,
Of markets, crowds, the press on the pavement,
Of fellow man and friend;
Of lovers in lamplight, millhands in the morning,
Miners, machinists, mates and chinas,
Company to earth's end.

I could praise the shy devoted heroes
Who, from the sky's awareness or the oceans',
Answer to Smith or Jones:
And those who wait, dread-heavy, for their homing,
For love and the bare charity of living,
Death in their bones.

Shall I write us a song with this for burden,
This dear lie of the land which blood enhances,
Seen with death in the eye?
Shall I celebrate our own, the trusting ones,
The fruitful-living daughters and sons
Beneath the aiming sky?

Song of the Chances of War

[1942]

O RINGING glass
    And drowning sailor.
Some go to war
With words on paper.
O whistled tune
And luckless airman.
Some go to war
Sheathed in a sermon.

Some are too wise
To think it over
Or grudge to lose
Sweet life, sweet lover.
And lucky ones
Of simple stature
Kill not to kill
But serve the future.

O ringing glass
O luckless whistle.
The weeds grow proud,
Day crowns the thistle.
Ill-luck and lack
Go sickle-handed.
Keen is the blade,
The eye most candid.

Happy-Go-Lucky

[1942]

HAPPY-GO-LUCKY he
      Heeded well
How shone the sun
·The day he fell.

No man his debtor, none
Heir to this
Bloom no woman raised
To earthly bliss.

Happy-go-lucky he
Gave but heed
To laughter and that kiss
Which children need.

Epitaph

[1942]

HE soared against the yielding air,
  He leant against the sky.
On earth the blossom froth of spring
Has scorched his inmost eye.
His teeth met in the summer fruit
And let the teeming waste
Of the abundant juices scald
His comprehending taste.
Now flesh which was as foliage,
Which was as fine and firm
As lustre of the holly leaf,
Is gutted with the worm.
It was a worm of discontent
With sap and sun and blood,
A worm with inner sightless eyes
Crept to him from the mud,
A worm that never saw the sky
Nor praised the lark-loud air,
But conned his shapely skeleton
And swept each bright bone bare.

Flight Above Cloud

[1 9 4 2]

WORDS form and fall. The body outsoars the brain.
England slides under, deep drowned with use and years
Words fall, to join their element again,
Empty and innocent as rain's fresh tears
Spun in this heavenly main.

Earth's toil and the soil, furrowed and fretted, exist
Only in the memory which gives no heed,
Locked in the skill of soaring eye and wrist,
At a mechanic instance freed
From the sure moralist.

I cannot name this air, this infinite span,
Unroofed, fitfully floored with clouds slow surge:
Nor for a likeness use for words the plan
Of earth moulded and wrought within the verge
And limit of seeing man.

Forty-Eight Hours

[1942]

WITH sudden ease,
    And Mozart played at night,
Lamplight upon brushed hair,
Wind leaf-lost in the trees,
I am aware
How man must pay with love.

With little spent
And life to pay away,
To-day, to-morrow, all
Are lost in the event:
And we are small,
All we who pay with love!

Crew Room

[1942]

BEYOND this disregard,
 The casual answer, and the hard
Brief pranks,
Is kindness which is metal
Patterned as stalk and petal,
As the wide flower frank.

Yet Fear and Death, abstract
And terrible as dreams, enact
The scene
Against which these stand gainly,
Living nobly or vainly,
Parting with casual mien.

Beyond some sum of words,
Some bashful imagery of birds
Are spun
Together out of laughter
More than the senses after
Ever will make of disregard or fun.

When Bullets Prove

[1942]

IN times when bullets prove, when deeds decide:
  Nor the cool laughter of the youthful corn
Nor brief hot poppies hide
Earth trodden and torn.

In times when smiling eyes and lips tell lies,
And only dead men tell no tales, no tales
Casting their last disguise,
Love alone avails.

Hold hard to the dear thought. For courage less
This tenderness is but a dress worn thin
Against the cold. Love's dress
Is blood-deep under the skin.

Training Flight

[1942]

THE Flying Instructor's voice is historic
  Speaking of airspeed, engine boost or trim,
Reckoning them all, but judging the human
Eye and eagerness: skill in head and limb.
The steady gist of words in the headphones
Is surely the voice of all, exploring flight,
All prophets, philosophers, students of reason,
Appraising how the man shall stay upright.

Roses and Ruins

[1942]

ONCE more the rose, rally of English heart,
  Blooms at the crater, at the ruined sill,
Where life left off, where love was left, where part
Of you or you stay still.

There is no public wrong or private grief
Can stain the colours, steal the proud design.
Autumn may snatch the petal and the leaf.
Now, the whole flower is yours and mine.

Lucky to live and greet the rose full blown,
Which blooms on death and flaunts the frightened hour;
To see the emblem of most inner bone
Clothed in the frail flesh of the flower.

Smith

[1942]

SMITH, living on air,
  Your astral body
  A mechanic wonder,
Your anger an affair
Of fire and thunder.

Smith, who puts down fear,
Whose young heart
Grapples with pity, whose spirit
Holds life on earth so dear,
And death no merit.

Missing

[1942]

LESS said the better.
  The bill unpaid, the dead letter,
No roses at the end
Of Smith, my friend.

Last words don't matter,
And there are none to flatter.
Words will not fill the post
Of Smith, the ghost.

For Smith, our brother,
Only son of loving mother,
The ocean lifted, stirred,
Leaving no word.

One Country-Bred

[1942]

DID Smith so love this land:
    May love of country still
Cradle the fretted heart
With wold and hill?

May Smith, one country-bred,
Have set a meadow round
The near horizons of
High sky and ground?

Did Smith still live to kill,
Recalling trees in bloom
And, entering into shade,
Smile at his doom?

So did Smith love this land,
So love of country will
Enforce a heart-weak hand
And ease the iron skill.

Sooner or Later

[1942]

SOONER or later, loss
And, cruellest of all winds, pity
Must blow across
My nature and my body's old resolve.

How shall I meet the blast,
The standstill of passion, winter
Of loss ice-fast:
And blood still blood that trims the will to live?

For better or for worse,
In laughter, in anger join me
When that adverse
Wind come.

I value this the most:
Companions with no more to lose,
That thrifty host
Which storms the barren times to live one hour.

Sooner or later, yet
Most lonely in all men, pity
Must still be met
Alone, perhaps in tatters at high noon.

Another Summer of War

[1 9 4 2]

O WAR is whispering in the barley,
   And green ears sweeten in the sun.
O with charlock and red poppy
Weed-proud summer is begun.

Summer too innocent in beauty
Strips the eye which wakes ashamed:
Drenching daylight with high lark-song
Where the very sky is aimed.

In a chastity of air, war ventures,
Where the rose forms innocently whole.
In the ardent pallor of the barley,
War sighs, fumbling for the soul.

The New Story

[1942]

LET the cold fire break out in happy men,
　Their blade the reasoning edge, their bomb the fury,
Outblast of understanding, force sudden,
Deliberate as surgery.

The gun within my head all fear shall stun.
The bombing eye shall look for peace not glory.
Be there no news of honour being won
But the beginning of a new story.

The fire, in man instinct, now coldly flares
Kindled from gutted hearth, from modest room
Open to skies, from love spent unawares
And little figures mustering for doom.

Limply the broadcast words balloon on air,
Stale as the comic jokes: now gunfire only
Is real: and the brief handclasps which must tear
The lonely from the lonely.

Fall

[1 9 4 2]

THE tale of war, the story,
   Same as rain, falls evenly on all:
And the words for honour and glory
Wear too small.
Too slight the words, and spoken
Too often, as sky and sight shake down,
The serene marble broken,
The stray shot killing child or clown.

Now autumn without pity
Burnishes all flesh and has no shame.
Lovers in wheat-field and in city
Make their claim.
O same as rain or seasons,
Falling, falling on lovers and all,
War falls, wastrel of rhyme and reason.
Honour and glory wear so small.

The Head's Secret

[1 9 4 2]

NO peace in the ruin.
No comfort in the dead.
Life lapsing in the body
Lives but in the head.

But seek you the last answer,
The final gout of grief:
This head replies with silence
Of an old belief.

No sign in bomb's dead litter,
No marvel in the sky:
But the head's secret only
Refuses to die.

Carol

[1942]

NOW peace on earth
  To taker, giver,
The thirsting sea,
The yielding river,
Bright sky steep up
From star to star.
O sleep too dear,
With love so far.

Now ancient peace
Seal off each eye
That all alone
As when men die
The nearer bone
Prepare to rest,
Within each night
A child as guest.

Nights in a Troopship

[1942]

O NARROW, narrow the world.
　　Here all hopes fuse
At the salt horizon of distance, danger:
Of what may pick and choose
From friend or stranger.

O sorry, sorry the sight
That bled our eyes
With the dear humdrum of homeland last sighted,
To bleach us with these skies
Curding and blighted.

For ever, ever love
Swills belly and brain
In those fast inners of each man who musters
Sleep-locked beneath the wain
Of tropic clusters.

As lonely, lonely the ships
In convoy keep
To a strict station on constellar courses,
Singly each man seeks sleep,
Each borne in his resources.

O sorry, sorry the world
That blighted all
These grave and delicate lives with grief unearned:
Who shine the more, being small,
For great hearts being burned.

Carol of the Children during War

[1942]

THEY take on trust
  This chaste and starry night,
Their dream so just;
Their childish thought so bright.

They move at last
Through silver-sward of fields.
To them all past
And darkest present yields.

Come Holy Ghost
With the same innocent motion,
To camp, field-post,
Man lone in air and ocean,

Where winter dearth,
The atrocity not cold,
Has stormed the last stronghold
Of body's earth.

That man may take on trust
The ancient holiness,
His dream as just,
As children's dreams, guileless.

Mid-Atlantic Blues

[1942]

My sheets are warm to-night
    Though Love must lie alone.
My sheets are warm and white:
And Love is not a stone,
Not cold and adamant,
Not to sink in the sea.
While blood is vigilant
Lies Love awake in me:
As wide as the sour swell
That menaces the soul,
As danger tolls the bell,
As fear's sunk steeples toll.
My love, warm well my bed
While war frets out in storm.
For Love, wide in this head,
Keep my sheets warm.

First Sighting of West Africa

[1943]

O UT of the swelling noon,
    Bursting the eye with tears of heat,
From the parched sea
Looms Africa.

O land of lions,
Of gold guarded by fevers,
Spinning a drapery of green sierras
From the sky's side.
Land, magic with favours,
Perilous with love,
Behind the garnish of the noble stance,
The wonderful ambush.

Travellers bring no peace,
But thirst and bibles:
Reaching pale medicated hands for more
Favours and gold,
Hard ivory, yielding slaves.
Spoilers for centuries have gained this coast,
Seeking a timeless agony of wealth,
Bright as a fever in the flickering night.

The African Aerodrome

[1943]

AGAIN, again, and again
  Where the light of day stood still
In a season without rain
In a land without a hill

You utter the magic names
Of the suburb or the field
With Saturday football games
Till the glassy light-walls yield,

Till you force the gold land's glaze
With a remembered gust
Of narrow windy days,
Till boots touch roots through dust.

Nor do you speak in vain
Where the light of day stands still
In a season without rain
In a land without a hill.

Air Convoy

[1943]

BIRD-WIDE the caravan
   Scorches through Africa,
Wary of the harmattan,
Wind of riven sand;
Blazing through the yellow haze
Or the sky's crass enmity,
Violent in the noon-maze
Of the yellow land;
Caravan of aeroplanes,
Sharp-beaked and positive,
Flickering above the stains
And ruts which mark mankind
Clearer than the animal
In the old adversity,
In the supernatural
Striving of a mind.

The Radio Word

[1 9 4 3]

SOUND-BRIGHT, from night to day, from noon to
    evening,
From the old hearth to the new fireside, friending
Future with past and man with man;
Over all sky-line, separation, ending,
Uprose this span.

These kindred heard the home bells in the prairie,
In jungle heard the tale, at sea the story,
And were alone no longer for words spoken
Binding the new hopes with an older glory,
For the outposted stillness broken.

So, engineered with light, this world span, now no
    wonder,
Forges the heart-link fast between men's reason,
Staving a world against the blast
At every moment. Truth, in every season
Here must speak steadfast.

Landscape: Western Desert

[1943]

WINDS carve this land
  And velvet whorls of sand
Annul footprint and grave
Of lover, fool, and knave.
Briefly the vetches bloom
In the blind desert room
When humble, bright, and brave
Met common doom.

Their gear and shift
Smother in soft sand-drift,
Less perishable, less
Soon in rottenness.
Their war-spent tools of trade
In the huge space parade:
And, with this last distress,
All scores are paid.

And who will see,
In such last anarchy
Of loveless lapse and loss
Which the blind sands now gloss,
The common heart which meant
Such good in its intent;
Such noble common dross
Suddenly spent.

Fleet Exercise

[1943]

IF action in itself could stay
   Salt blood which never slakes that thirst
Which the head has
And which the eye sees first:

If deeds so lovely were enough,
If purity in form was grace,
If bodies had
The good to match the face;

A swift device of flight would salve
The threat which keeps the heart in dread,
Such tall fine ships
Would justify the dead.

Graves: Tobruk

[1943]

LIVE and let live.
   No matter how it ended,
These lose and, under the sky,
Lie friended.

For foes forgive,
No matter how they hated,
By life so sold and by
Death mated.

Malta

[1943]

DISTANTLY, by navigator's calculation
Pinpointing rock in the waters, the target
Mistily seen through the panels of air's dimension.
A point or so to starboard. That's there all right.
The expected, our landfall, Malta.

Look! Malta spun on the sea, shaping to sight
Fragilely as a promise, framed by metal
And the deft handling of airmanship.
Nudge. Nod. That's there all right. A petal
Yellow, all veined with green in the sea's hard
Flooring of other element, of timeless running.
Malta, upon the blood-invested water, cactus, nettle-
Leafed, old prickle, guard.

Fly in to circuit the runways, scarred
And scored sparsely on land hard-won,
Beaten out amid ridges and walls like wrinkles
In ancient faces sweetened by the sun.
From lofts of air, here hover over the stones
Fashioned and catacombed, lidding the eye that twinkles
And watches with Phoenician patience over the years,
Casting a count of nations' dust and bones.
Not much of a size, this rock. Some nine by seventeen.
O witness to the Mediterranean glory, to the tears,
And the learning and the swagger. All watched: all seen.

Now circuit once the sallow veined-with-green
Pale rock, pale builded block, flushed dome and steeple,
The monuments of saints, the dappled lemon groves,
The air-bleached mannerisms of baroque,
And the jet shadows on the roads of people:
By Saint Paul guided, by the stone folds of bastions
    guarded,
Tillers and toilers, minders of scanty droves,
So little needed new, so much less old discarded,
In poor tilth found, in timeless age provided.
Wheels down. Full flaps: and glide to ground.
Phoenician-eyed, these saw Carthage and Rome,
Greeks, Infidels and Normans in their humours:
Nor shall we rouse them when these engines sound
Along the ruthless skyline of an aerodrome.

Death is our mission and, at the long last, home,
Unshadowed by the killing, by the organic wrong,
Unawed by glory or the mice-whispers of fear.
Home we desire, and the most of us young, armed, strong,
With these weapons proving an older integrity,
No bolder for death being near.
Watch the old eyes now, like the clang of the bell
In your sleep or the sirens of an alert
Deep in your body's keep of silence. Watch them well:
These work hard, these peasants, scratching at dirt,
And take little notice of flying. Older, stranger,
One here saw Carthage dying, lying under the plough:

One here saw Tyrian Astoreth, lusting, fall;
One here saw Rome in danger;
One faltered, knelt at the shipwreck of Saint Paul.

Jack Airman, at leisure now, no avenger,
With a whatsyours and the silken popsy reclining
On fancy's cushion, no killing
To ward off happiness, no challenger shining,
The mission is death. Your careful lining
And personal armoury saves you whole
From the too-dear erosion, love or friendship,
From the parting, the too-long-lingering, the confusion
Of grief and loving life. No toll
Ever was taken but here these eyes looked on,
And the waters were troubled with blood and oil.
Death blooms in Mediterranean profusion:
We are old where nothing is new, now, Airman John.

Zeppu* leans over against the soil,
Where airscrews', ailerons' pattern throws
Our emblem on the light of evening. Easily
Moves man ploughing, in meagreness, furrows
Watered and terraced by ancient husbandry.
Not all by Saints and Powers, Zeppu knows
—It's wonderful what people will believe—
How night or death assemble in the light,
How bean crops bloom or blemish, how the rose,
Most precious birth-rose in a bowl of water,
Smile or grieve.

* *Zeppu and Grez are a popular personification of the Maltese
peasant and his wife.*

Not many of them killed, considering. Just those
By law of average. Zeppu will forget
And Grez, barefooted, carrying her shoes,
Will pray for some till harvest. If we set
A time and limit to our fear. A time to choose,
A limit for the body's luck against the force
Of bombardment by thought and deed and thought;
We might be bold with the old eyes. We might not lose
Our singleness for fear of being caught.

So they trampled the Three Cities about the port,
And Valetta built by gentlemen for gentlemen, and the
    quays
And the garnished churches, and the alleys of stairs
Where noble quarterings passed which could not be
    bought,
And rooms where parchments faded with the family
    trees.
So that the carven limestone of the little houses
Clogs the fair prospects, stumbles on to squares,
Wind in an elegiac chandelier carouses,
A brocaded remnant curdles upon the breeze.
Knights, galley slaves, middlemen, pimps, corsairs
Contributed dust to dust, the yellow volley to heaven,
The must and reek of smoke that pillared and settled
Over the old waters, blood-invested, unawares.

No more the young man's hunger for the marvellous
    seas
Or the air's stairs and extremes is set and sealed

By sixteen knightly quarterings, tempered and mettled,
By the gilt character upon the azure field.
I see the legion of common men inherit
The rubble, the grandeur of the arches, and the shield
Of sight in the abysses, of Saint John, of lightning
In the righteous sky. Nor is there merit,
(Seen by that older eye which never perishes,)
Except by faith, by friends, by love, by country,
Cleansing and firing and brightening.

A lunar knife embellishes,
The old Renaissance fever burns
Its character of ice and gold on palaces.
Midnight so rare and bountiful returns;
Equally carving the knightly emblem,
The cross and the shield with light,
Describing the pattern of the chasm
Or the strangled flight,
Printed on air by the maimed balustrade;
Mercifully glossing cratered hearts with shade.

The mission is death. There is no shorter, longer
Entry over the old water where the sorry and the afraid
Are comfortable. There is no city,
Airman John, where in some chromium logic, man is
        stronger
Than man. There is no release from pity,
The skewer at the heart.
There is soil the foot treads after
The high-flying, the expert precision in space,

The careful briefing, the dicing, the laughter.
In the last rubble and beauty of the place,
An eye, hot, living, looks from a secret face.

We will fly away one day
And get us back to our homes and to the grace
Of tenderness, the sap which moves in the wood,
The balance of the head upon the daffodil,
The truth which was understood
In our indeterminate passion,
In the Saturday street or under the hill.
In our own fashion
We will be at peace and be still.
Jack Airman, if there be destiny for good
Among us, you have the power, the prowess, navi-
    gator's skill.
We will fly away one day with no need to kill.

Waterfront Ballad

[1 9 4 3]

SOME say it isn't deep
But it's deep enough for me.
Don't write no address on my grave
But the Mediterranean Sea.

I shan't drift in to shore:
For they'll pickle me a treat.
And I shall walk in a tidy rig
Past the ships of many a fleet.

Ships you never heard of,
Fleets that went down in thunder:
And them old shipmates from all the wars
Sharing the Mediterranean plunder.

Royal Air Force Anniversary

[1 9 4 3]

FITTERS and riggers, draughtsmen and engineers,
All, names and unknown, who fashioned this force,
Let us consider twenty-five years;
Time for the building of a body's plenty,
Time for a wrist to thicken,
Time for the precious third of a life to run its course
In times, threat-crowded, loud with fears,
The mechanic urge, with your whole craft, has brought
    to quicken
A weapon of light, of no-horizon-pent resource.

Pilots, navigators, gunners and aircraft crew,
All you acclaimed and nameless ones, whose skill
With instruments, the compass, the plain rhythms of
    morse,
With aerobatics, landings, with the stooge's patience
Flying on and on, beyond frontiers, daylight's sill,
Beyond caring, beyond hill or valley you knew
And treasured as your lasting thought, as home.
Let us consider these twenty-five years, your lifetime's
    third,
And see from the levelled pattern of an aerodrome
The easy envied passage of a bird.

Yours is the instrument, the traffic of air.
Its magic has caught you, and gifted you and your like,

Caparisoned you with the power to swoop and strike,
Not heroes, but apprentices in the trade
And traffic of airmanship, a just rule understood.
Into your hands is this fell weapon laid;
Not for the dark terror, a blind stabbing in the shade,
But for the power, in the ordinary men and women,
    for good.

The Lily Lulling Me Away

[1943]

THE lily lulling me away
  From Africa with petals molten white,
Poured upon night,
Assembles, in a silence, abstract themes,
The heart's most tenderest devices,
The forgotten-in-the-morning dreams.

The lily lulling me away
From a war's camouflage of khaki thought
Is making sport,
Abandoning disquiet like sullied dress,
War's sable cloth upon the senses
Stripped for the chastity of tenderness.

Ballad Under the Atlas

[1943]

THE lad with the bruise on his lip
Sleeps lightly, so little spoilt, so little kissed,
A blemish so quickly mended.
How much, in time for loving, has he missed
Lying alone, unfriended?

Under the Atlas, the pillars
Underpinning the fall of the ancient sky,
Under that prop of thunder,
Why do they let him, alone, unfriended, lie
For one to pause, to see a bruise, and wonder?

Now the wounded, mock heroic
Survivors to smiles, to honour, to a pain
Of pity in the eyes of mothers,
Sweethearts and strangers, are moved again.
But why don't they take him on with the others?

He died, did the lad with the bruise,
That's why. His body inside him raddled with blast:
His bruised lip not to be mended,
All spoiling and kissing past,
Lying alone, unfriended.

O where are pillars, the shoulders
Holding the sky up now, withstanding the fall!
O where the might, the girder

Of light, the wholeness lit in that lowering pall
Fouling the features of earth and air with murder!

The lad with the bruise on his lip,
All these ones, so little spoilt, so lightly lent:
Are the holders,
And little, in time for loving, will they have spent,
Unaware of the light held up by their shoulders.

Song: Tripoli to Algiers

[1943]

TO-DAY the sky shook out:
  Hilariously the high airs
Tumbled and trembled
As if their element
Would have us unawares.

The honey-mountains, hills
And fretted lakes, all salted stiff,
Moon-made, firm frills
Of dream-deep valley,
Lunar cliff,

Slewed, sheered away below.
And we, stable upon a course,
Rode through the trackless sky
With human, apt precision
Borne between mind and force.

Central Park Blues

[1 9 4 3]

SWING it, Manhattan,
  Swing me the blues of material progress.
Swing me the song of the body's prosperity.
Swing me a pattern,

Manhattan, a blues,
A song of to-night and damn to-morrow,
A thousand spires of song in sky's white clarity,
Loud-beat, gong-bright news,

Blues, a breaking story
With an old Jack's-as-good-as-his-master theme,
The poet's dream crowding Manhattan. O city
Foul with man's glory.

Casualty

[1943]

ONE sang in the evening
   Before the light was gone:
And the earth was lush with plenty
Where the sun shone.

The sound in the twilight
Went: and the earth all thin
Leans to a wind of winter,
The sun gone in:

One song the less to sing
And a singer less
Who sleeps all in the lush of plenty
And summer dress.

Truce

[1943]

WHEN you are through with wrong,
  Come, killer boy, come empty-handed,
When you have spat the sun out with a song.

Come empty-handed then:
Come, crack-brained home: come, sightless glory,
Into the crowding hearts of men.

When you are through with wrong,
Have fouled the moon with a mean story
Stay on to cheer amid the cheering throng.

Elegy for Tom Roding

[1943]

AFTER the death spelt out in headlines, after the gains
　　Broadcast by the dispassionate voices,
Comes word to a village.
Loss with the lifted latch. With poor remains
Of the meal unfinished comes pillage
And ruin upon the country hearts of some.
The small death come,
And poor the sorrow shared by a few.

Not along with the old people beneath the yew
Lying at peace, not with those old
Comfortable ones sharing God's acre of ground,
Will he snore snug down under grass
For the idle and the children to pause and pass,
Hearing the enviable sound
Of the wind in the yew,
The wind in the yew.

Tom Roding, tractor driver, of Slare
In the County of Essex, son of the dew
And misted hedgerows, minder of riddies,
Comrade of the autumnal hare
Tawny upon the stubble. Lost to these widest skies,
Clodhopper, clay-built, your still eyes
Viewing unnameable Armageddon, lost one,
One of the casualties, old George Roding's son.

News is written in blood and the radio words
Entering a cottage parlour are charged with lives.
Over Eazle Wood homes evening with the homing birds:
And summer listens to the gaffers and to the old wives.
No doubt there will be some village memorial.
There will be names cut for all to recall.
And the few who knew Tom Roding will fall
To their few regrets at evening, with the chill of the dew
And the wind in the yew,
The wind in the yew.

So was one life spent, of many,
In a mouthful of sand in desert in the bare
Vengeful enemy sunlight. For Jenny,
For Alice, for Flo with evening sound
Of homing birds is heart-loss, sorrow. At Slare
Come settle the sum of Tom Roding, tractor driver,
      heir
To widest sky, corn-ripple, harvest dew,
His saved wealth fifteen pound.
And O the wind in the yew,
The wind in the yew.

A Billet in Naples Bay

[1 9 4 3]

WHAT gutted eye shall paint
The beautiful seasons now?
Shall brightest day become a lust
For hasting hands at wheels, at triggers
Anxious under the flowering bough?

O shall chrysanthemums'
Autumnal earth-scent fall
Upon a wounded tongue that fears
Winter and lack of home and only
Dreads love most of all?

Peace be with us at last
With wintery eye or just
Zealous wide eye of spring to see
Flesh in the flower, in lips, in fingers, fast
Beyond the easy bullet's lust.

Calvary

[1 9 4 3]

WITH them dies hope.
    With every one, blood-shod,
Resolute in the lovely mechanism,
Intuitive in poise with life and death,
Falls one before God.

Oh Christ if hope
Shall die with each of these
Innocent in the content of the heart,
Martyrdom of nails and unjust laws were vain,
Sinners were strung from trees.

Fair Warning

[1 9 4 3]

TAKE care
    Sun's prodigal
Whose metal acid air
At last will eat,
Will threaten the heart's centre
Where love's old cunning heat
Also may enter.

Take heed
Life's realist
Your aptitude for deed,
Final and fast,
May fall to need for rapture:
Your love at last
Be easy capture.

Revenge

[1943]

WHO said revenge?
  The blind eye at the sights;
Lips, bloodied, crushed;
The old who pray at nights;
The white child hushed?

Whose vengeance proves?
 Graves, nameless, innocent;
God on our side;
The hapless dead content;
And no more pride?

The eye that killed,
Lips that desired the kiss,
The young and old
Were innocent in this.
Revenge is cold.